For my Mother

I want to thank my husband, Dave, and my children, Vivian and Harold, for their patience, help, and honest criticism.

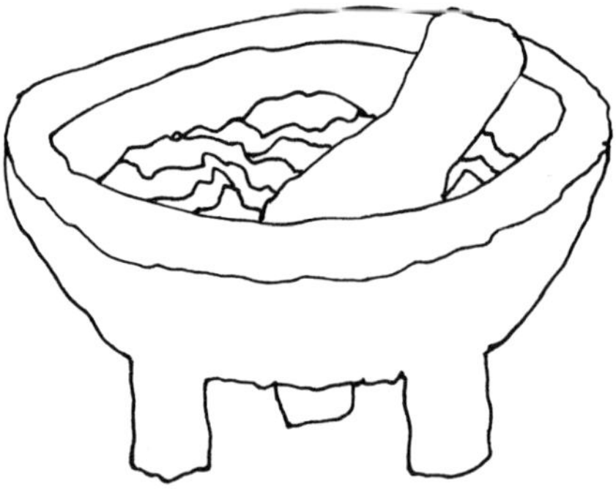

CONTENTS

Esther Gonzales Davis

INTRODUCTION

I am happy to say that the little cookbook of my favorite recipes, that I put together in my home two years ago, has pleased so many people that I have been asked to publish this second edition. This gave me a good chance to go over all the recipes and add some more of my very favorites.

I am often asked how I happened to write a cookbook. It all started when I was asked to teach Mexican cooking to a group in the Naval Officers' Wives Club. My first class, limited to ten, was held in my kitchen. The class grew, and we had to move to a larger kitchen. I began teaching the basic steps in Mexican cooking—and that is what my cookbook is all about: basic recipes, geared to the beginner.

After a few classes, June Baldwin, one of my students, said, "Esther, you should write a cookbook and share your recipes with us and others."

Well, to be honest, at the time I had mixed emotions. Could I part with all my recipes? (You cooks out there know what I'm talking about.) After all, these dishes had been taught to me by my mother and grandmother when I was learning how to cook as a child. None of the recipes was written down on paper, and nothing was ever measured by teaspoons or cups; always a pinch of this and a pinch of that. The hardest part of putting this book together was learning how to measure the ingredients.

I was born in Yorktown, Texas, and grew up in Corpus Christi, in a family of nine children. I was the oldest girl in the family, and I had more responsibilities than the other girls. I was taught to cook; it was my job to teach the others. By the age of ten I could cook a whole meal by myself.

One incident from my girlhood I will always remember. I had prepared a meal for the family, and one of the dishes was boiled beans. After a while, my father said, "I think we need a fishing pole." Not knowing what he meant, my mother asked, "What for?"

"So that I can go fishing for these beans," answered my father. "I can't seem to catch any with the spoon." We all had a good laugh, and ate the beans as soup.

In my cooking today, I try to retain the methods and flavors I learned as a girl. I freeze very little, and will not cook many of my dishes ahead of time. Mexican food needs to be served hot.

I have had to make changes in some of my recipes, because of using commercial products, but by all standards the food is still as tasty as when I was a child.

My husband and children are still my best critics as I work on my recipes and prepare foods. If they don't like something, out it goes.

I have received so many letters from women who have purchased the book, and these letters are more rewarding to me than all the money in the world. I would like to share a few with you.

One woman wrote: "I used your cookbook to plan a dinner, and the food was delicious. Since I've been trying to cook Mexican food for my husband for 10 years, he was very pleased I was finally successful, thanks to your good directions."

Another letter from a young woman brought tears to my eyes, and made all my efforts worthwhile. She wrote, "I was so happy with your recipes. I've seen hundreds of recipes for Mexican food, but I never thought they sounded good. Yours were like my grandmother's taste. She is gone now and never wrote anything down....I have been trying to recapture the flavor she put into her food. I feel like I'm learning from a friend when I read your recipes....Thank you so much for this feeling of joy...."

Good luck and happy cooking,

ESTHER'S HELPFUL HINTS

All stirring should be done with a wooden spoon.

A little flour sprinkled in the frying pan after butter or oil is heated will prevent eggs from sticking.

Placing onions in the freezer for at least 5 minutes, and a little lemon squeezed on the cutting board, will cut down on those tears.

Garlic is very potent in flavor, and one should take care in deciding how much is enough to use. Too much garlic can ruin a dish; always use in moderation.

Always cook garlic slowly. If you desire more flavor, crush clove before cooking. Do not let garlic stand too long or it will become dry and tasteless. Fresh garlic will keep longer if stored in airtight glass jar in the refrigerator.

Remember that the amounts of any spice to be used in cooking can always be adjusted to suit one's individual taste.

Whenever steaks are pan-fried, save those rich juices for making delicious gravies or to be used in place of bouillon. Add one cup warm water to pan and allow to cool, then pour in jar. Place in refrigerator. Fat will separate from stock; when using the stock, discard all fat.

Always buy whole chicken. Do not throw away pieces such as neck, wings, etc. These make excellent chicken broth for cooking, and may be frozen in ice cube trays and stored in plastic bags in the freezer. When you need chicken broth, just use the ice cubes.

I also make vegetable broth ice cubes from the outer leaves of vegetables one would ordinarily discard. Wash them thoroughly, cook in a little water, then freeze the drained liquid in ice cube trays and store in plastic bags. These add more flavor than plain water when added to soups or other dishes.

Longhorn cheese may be substituted if jack cheese is not available.

Saffron is a seasoning and coloring, but it is important to note that Mexican saffron and Spanish saffron come from two different plants and are NOT interchangeable.

Prior to the initial use of the molcajete, grind in it ¼ cup of raw rice, until the inside of the mortar and the bottom of the pestle are smooth. It will be necessary to repeat this process 3 or 4 times, or until there is no evidence of loose grit. Wash thoroughly.

If you cannot find a molcajete, you can use a mortar and pestle for grinding ingredients. A blender can be used also, but be very careful to blend only briefly, or you will end up with puree!

A round length of wood, or dowel, 1½ inches in diameter and 6-7 inches long, is an excellent rolling pin for making tortillas. This can be made to order at any lumber yard.

Cilantro will keep longer if you do not remove stems after cleaning. Keep in an airtight container or wrap well. Try not to cut the cilantro with a knife; instead, tear gently as you would any fresh green. Why not grow your own from coriander seeds sold in the spices section if you cannot find cilantro in your market?

Whipped lard is called for in tamale and empanada recipes. Before whipping lard allow it to stand at room temperature for at least an hour, and use it at room temperature.

ABOUT CHILES

When handling hot chiles, keep your hands away from your face, and especially your eyes. Wash hands thoroughly afterwards.

The hottest part of the chile is the seed. Normally seeds are discarded, except in hot sauce. For a hotter flavor, leave some of them in. Fresh chiles may be soaked for an hour or so in cold water and salt to remove some hotness.

To peel chiles, see page 48.

ancho A mild-flavored, 3-inch-long pepper that resembles the bell pepper, but is more pointed in shape and darker in color. Most often available dried, in the Mexican spice section of supermarkets; sometimes called "Mexican chiles." Dried anchos are dark red or black.

California Also called "Anaheim" chile. The most commonly available chile, green when ripe and red when dried. It is 5-8 inches long, and 1-1½ inches in diameter. This is the chile I refer to as a "fresh green chile" in my recipes for Chiles Rellenos and Repollos Rellenos. Also available canned, called "whole chiles" or "green chiles." (If the can says "hot chiles," it contains jalapeño peppers.)

chile powder Many variations are available; some are a blend of ground chiles and other spices, some are pure chile. They range from mild to very hot—experiment to find your favorite.

jalapeños Green tapered chiles, about 2 inches long. These are hot, probably the most widely available hot peppers. They come fresh, canned, and pickled.

mulato Larger than the ancho and a bit hotter, this chile is available dried, often labeled "Mexican chiles." Can combine with or substitute for the ancho or pasilla.

pasilla A long, thin pepper, dark green when immature, brown when ripe or dried. It is 6-10 inches long and 1 or 2 inches in diameter. Mild in flavor and can be interchanged with the ancho or mulato, as you may not be able to find all three.

red peppers, dried These can be of many different varieties, widely available in the spice section of markets. They are quite hot, so you may wish to soak them in boiling water for 30 minutes and drain them before using.

serrano Small green (red or yellow when ripe) tapered peppers about 1½ inches long. These are tasty and hot. Most often found canned or pickled. If you can't find them, use jalapeños.

yellow wax These hot peppers come either fresh or pickled. There are several varieties, and they are interchangeable.

GLOSSARY

bolillo	small roll like a French roll
chorizo	highly seasoned Mexican sausage
cilantro	fresh coriander leaves, also known as Chinese parsley. Found with the parsley and watercress in grocery stores.
comal	iron griddle for cooking tortillas
comino	cumin, seed or powder
fideos	coils of very fine vermicelli
harina	flour
manteca	lard; super for making tamales and flour tortillas
masa	MASA HARINA is made from dried corn which has been soaked in lime water and cooked and ground. INSTANT MASA is commercially produced masa harina for making corn tortillas and tamales; available in grocery stores. FRESH MASA, which contains water, can be purchased in any tortilla factory. It must be used right away; it does not keep. Instant masa weighs less since it is dry; when wet it will almost double in weight. If my recipe calls for 10 pounds of masa, I'm speaking of fresh masa. Therefore use less instant masa for the recipe.
molcajete	stone mortar and pestle for grinding spices and chiles. To cure a new molcajete, see Esther's Helpful Hints.
piloncillo	small cone-shaped loaf of unrefined brown sugar, found with Mexican spices in stores. Also called *panocha.*
salsa	sauce, especially refers to hot sauce.

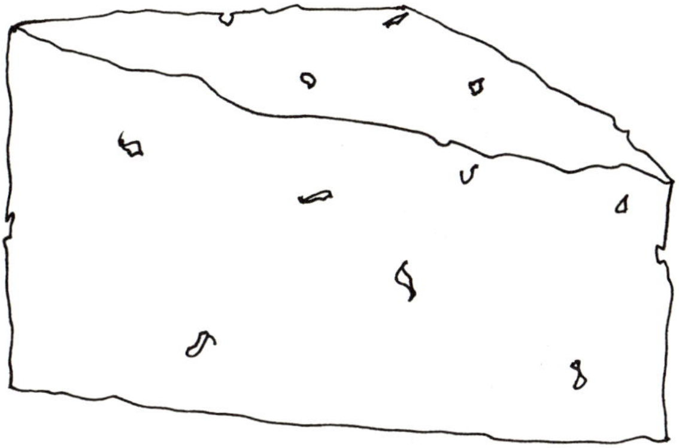

APERITIVOS
APPETIZERS

TOSTADA CHIPS

1-2 dozen corn tortillas
1 cup corn oil
salt

Tear each tortilla into eight pieces. Drop 10 to 12 pieces at a time into very hot oil. Cook until golden brown and crisp. Drain on a paper towel, and salt while still warm. Repeat this process until all pieces are cooked.

Serve with bean dip, guacamole, and with chile sauce.

QUESADILLAS

Mexican Grilled Cheese

corn or flour tortillas
jack cheese
fresh or canned peeled roasted chile
 peppers (optional)

Quesadillas may be made with either corn or flour tortillas. Lay a tortilla on a heated skillet. Place jack cheese, grated or in strips, in the center and fold. Cook on both sides until the cheese is melted.

Any cheese of your choice may be used. Canned or fresh chile peppers may be added as the cheese is melting.

APERITIVO DE FRIJOLES CALIENTES

Hot Bean Dip

2 cups cooked pinto beans (see recipe page 34)
3 jalapeños, well-mashed
¼ cup jack cheese, grated

Drain beans, reserving liquid. Mash beans with a potato masher, adding enough liquid to obtain desired consistency. Heat over low heat, adding mashed jalapeños and cheese.

Serve hot from a chafing dish with tostada chips (page 18) or commercial corn chips.

Yields 2 cups of Aperitivo de Frijoles.

Note: Whenever one of my recipes calls for jalapeños, use canned jalapeños.

GUACAMOLE

This guacamole dip is my favorite. I have tried other guacamoles but always come back to my original recipe.

2	soft ripe avocados
½-1	cup sour cream
1	small minced onion
1	ripe minced tomato
1	teaspoon lemon juice
¼	teaspoon garlic powder
¼	teaspoon oregano
¼	teaspoon ground comino
1	teaspoon salt
¾	teaspoon ground red peppers or 2 minced fresh chile peppers

Mash avocados and blend with sour cream. Add other ingredients. Cover. This dip can be served right away, but it will benefit if it stands for an hour or overnight.

Serve as a dip, as a salad, or with guacamole tacos (page 54), or tostada chips (page 18).

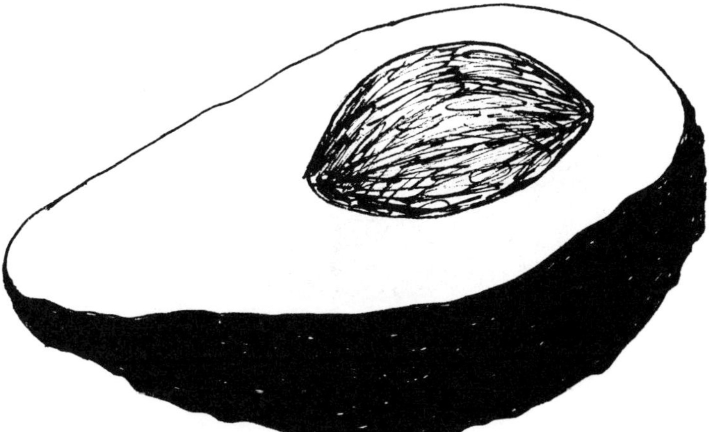

MARINATED CARROTS

These may be served as a relish or as an appetizer.

3 ounces of juice from a jar of hot jalapeño peppers
3-4 fresh carrots, diced
1 medium onion, diced
salt to taste

Blanch carrots and onion. Drain. Pour jalapeño juice over warm vegetables. Cover and store in refrigerator until completely chilled or overnight. Drain; do not serve juice.

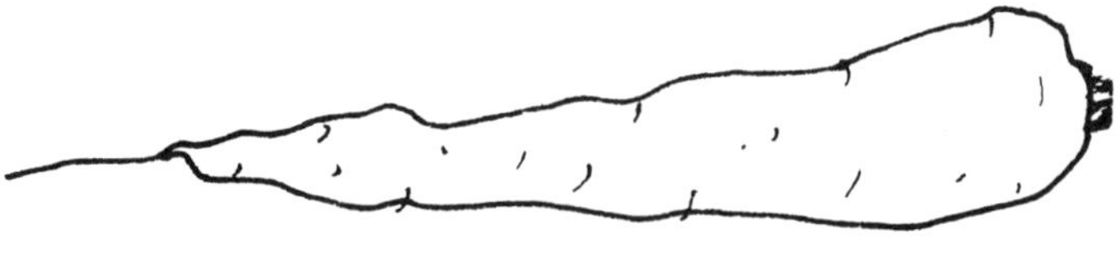

CHALUPITAS

"Little Boats"

When you become proficient in handling it, form the dough into little canoe-shaped boats.

1 pound fresh masa (see Glossary, page 16)
1 teaspoon salt
water

Combine the masa and salt with enough water to hold the dough together. Form dough into small balls. Make an indentation in the center of each ball with your finger.

Deep fry in hot oil until golden brown; keep warm in oven until all are fried. Fill with any meat of your choice, or with frijoles or cheese.

Makes approximately 60 Chalupitas.

CHILE CON QUESO

Chile with Cheese

1 small onion
1 tablespoon butter
1 can peeled roasted green chiles
4 ounces cream cheese
½ cup cream
salt and pepper to taste

Sauté onion in butter. Add chiles. Salt and pepper to taste. Simmer for 10 minutes. Add cream cheese, stirring until all of the cheese is melted. Add cream and remove from heat.

Serve in chafing dish to keep warm, with tostada chips (page 18) or commercial corn chips.

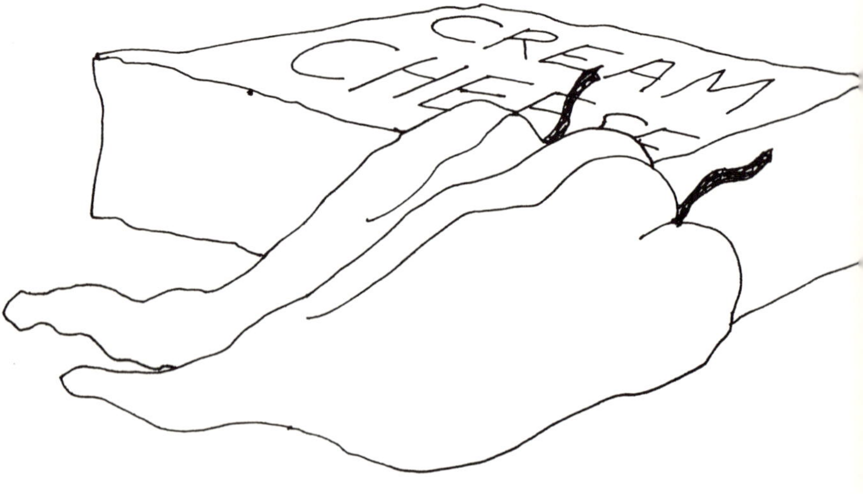

BUÑUELOS

The Appetizer

1 package large flour tortillas
½ cup finely grated jack or cheddar cheese
¾ cup corn oil
diced green chile peppers, if desired

Fry tortillas, one at a time, in hot oil until golden brown and crisp. Drain on paper towels. Sprinkle with grated cheese, and peppers if desired. Break into pieces for eating.

NACHOS

1 package corn tortillas
1 cup cooking oil
1-2 cups shredded jack, cheddar, or other cheese
1 can diced California green chiles
salt

Cut tortillas into wedges as for a pie, then fry pieces in hot oil to a golden brown. Sprinkle lightly with salt. Place wedges on a flat baking sheet. Sprinkle with cheese and peppers. Place pan in preheated 375° oven or under broiler until cheese melts. Serve at once.

CARNE ASADA

Roasted Meat

These appetizers disappear in no time!

2 pounds lean beef or pork
½ teaspoon garlic powder
salt and pepper to taste

Oven Method

Preheat oven to 350°. Cut meat into ½-inch cubes. Sprinkle with salt, pepper, and garlic powder. Bake in a shallow open pan for 1 hour. Shake pan occasionally to prevent meat from sticking.

Grill Method

Cut meat into ½-inch-wide strips. Sprinkle with salt, pepper, and garlic powder. Insert skewer, twisting meat as you insert it. Cook on charcoal grill or hibachi to desired degree of doneness. Serve hot.

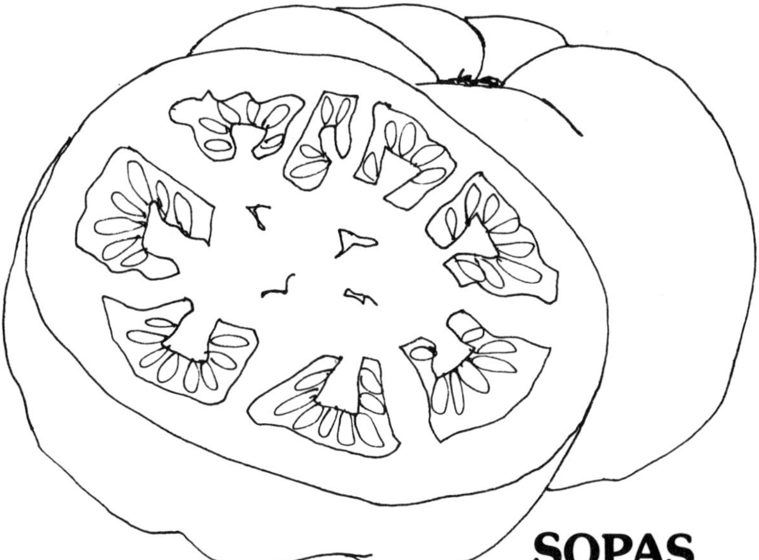

SOPAS
SOUPS

SOPA DE VERDURA

Vegetable Soup

2-3 ears fresh corn
4 cups beef stock
1 garlic clove
½ head cabbage
1 cup chopped onion
1 cup green bell pepper, chopped
2 tomatoes, chopped and peeled
2 potatoes, chopped
½ teaspoon oregano
1 bay leaf
1 teaspoon salt
1 teaspoon fresh ground black pepper
1 pound lean beef, cut in cubes
2 carrots, diced
½ pound zucchini, diced

Cut whole ears of corn into 1- to 2-inch pieces. Simmer garlic in olive oil until brown. Place all vegetables except carrots and zucchini in beef stock. Add seasonings and meat. Bring to a fast boil, then cook over low heat for 40 minutes. Add carrots and zucchini and cook an additional 20 minutes.

Serves 6.

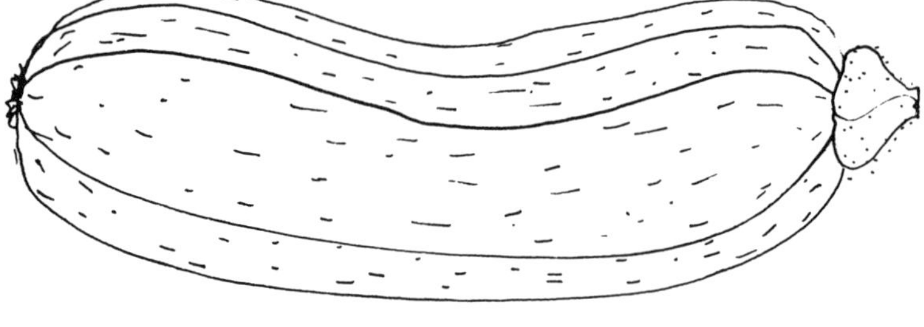

ALBONDIGAS

Meatball Soup

If you should ever make Albondigas without cilantro, you'll find it just doesn't taste right. You will become a believer in the use of spices.

2 cups potatoes
2 cups zucchini
¼ cup fresh cilantro
1 cup minced canned tomatoes or 1 8-ounce can tomato sauce
8 cups boiling water
1 pound ground beef
1 egg
salt and pepper to taste
1 cup instant rice
1 large onion, coarsely chopped
2 cups chopped carrots

Cut potatoes and zucchini into 1-inch cubes. Set aside until the last 15 minutes of cooking. Wash cilantro carefully and tear into small pieces by hand.

Mix beef, egg, salt, and pepper. Taking one pinch of each of the meat mixture, cilantro, rice, and onion, form into balls about one inch in diameter. Drop into rapidly boiling water to which tomatoes or tomato sauce have been added. Cook for 5 minutes.

Add potatoes and simmer for 15 minutes. Add zucchini and carrots, simmer 15 minutes longer.

Serve with hot corn or flour tortillas. Yields 6 servings of Albondigas.

Note: When I'm in a rush, I mix all the meatball ingredients together before forming them into balls. This speeds up the preparation.

SOPA DE POLLO

Chicken Soup

- 1 2-pound chicken, cut up, or 1 package (5 or 6) thighs
- 1 large onion, chopped
- 4 stalks celery, diced
- 1 clove garlic
- salt and pepper to taste
- 2½ quarts cold water
- 4 carrots, diced
- ½ cup rice
- 2 cubed potatoes
- ½ head cabbage cut into 8-10 wedges
- ¼ cup fresh chopped cilantro

Rinse chicken, combine with onion, celery, garlic, salt and pepper in cold water. Bring to fast boil, reduce heat, and cook until chicken is done (30-40 minutes). Cook carrots and rice separately. If instant rice is used, follow package instructions, cutting cooking time in half, and set aside. Cook carrots 3-5 minutes until tender. While these two are cooking, add diced potatoes and cabbage to the chicken soup, and cook until they are done. Then add carrots, rice, and cilantro and simmer 5 minutes more.

Serves 6-8.

SOPA DE PAPAS Y CARNE

Potato and Meat Soup

This was one of our standbys at home when I was growing up, and it still is, in our home today. Note that it can be made in two ways:

3 tablespoons oil or lard
6 potatoes, cut in ¼ inch slices
1 pound ground beef
salt and pepper to taste
2 tablespoons chile powder and 2-3 cups water
OR
1 small can tomato sauce and 2 whole wax chile peppers

Fry potatoes in oil for about 5 minutes. Add meat and fry, then add 1)chile powder and water, OR 2)tomato sauce and wax chiles. Salt and pepper to taste. Simmer until potatoes are cooked.

Serve with flour tortillas. This may be served as a soup or as a main dish.

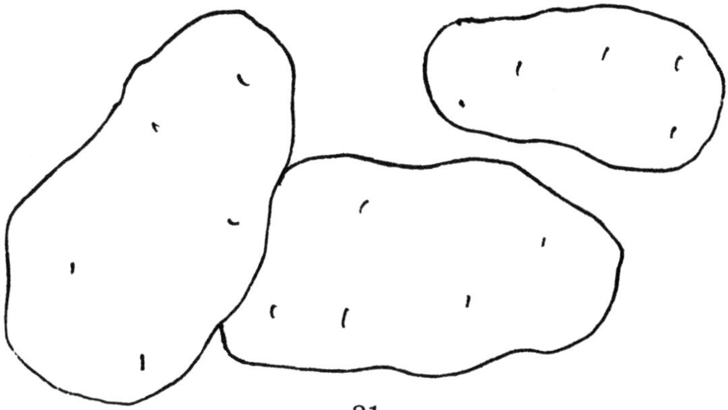

SOPA DE FIDEOS

Soup with Vermicelli

This is one of our "Sopas Secas" or dry soups. They're called "dry" because most of the water has been steamed out of them. Fideos are coils of very fine vermicelli.

1 tablespoon oil or bacon drippings
6 fideos
¼ teaspoon ground comino
¼ teaspoon garlic powder
1 cup tomato sauce
2 cups water or chicken broth
1 large slice of onion
2 bell pepper rings

Brown fideos in hot oil carefully to avoid breaking coils. Add the tomato sauce, broth, and seasonings.

Arrange onion slice and bell pepper slices on top of mixture. Cook slowly. Occasionally, stir gently. Sopa will be done when the liquid is almost gone.

Serve as a side dish with frijoles and flour tortillas. Yields 4 servings of Sopa de Fideos.

FRIJOLES
BEANS

FRIJOLES EN OLLA

Pot Beans; Pinto Beans

Frijoles freeze beautifully!

3 cups dried pinto beans
1 medium onion
1 garlic clove
½ teaspoon ground comino
small piece salt pork
1 teaspoon sugar
salt and pepper to taste
water

Wash beans thoroughly. The beans will be more flavorful if soaked overnight, but may be cooked right away. Put beans in pan with a large amount of water—enough to reach two inches above the beans. Add salt pork, whole onion, whole garlic clove, and all of the seasonings. Bring to a fast boil, then simmer for at least two hours or until the beans are soft to the touch when you press them between finger and thumb. Add water as needed during cooking. When beans are done, remove the onion and garlic.

Add sliced fresh onion and grated cheese and serve as a side dish, with hot corn or flour tortillas.

Yields 8 to 9 cups of frijoles.

Note: Slightly burned beans should be removed immediately from heat, drained, and transferred to another pot of hot water. Add one raw potato cut in half and resume cooking. Potato is to be removed after the beans are cooked.

FRIJOLES REFRITOS

Refried Beans

4 cups cooked pinto beans (page 34)
¾ cup bacon drippings or lard

In heavy skillet heat lard or bacon drippings. Add drained beans and mash with a potato masher. Continue cooking, stirring frequently, until all traces of fat have been absorbed.

Yields 4 to 6 servings.

FRIJOLES REFRITOS CON QUESO

Refried Beans with Cheese

4 cups cooked pinto beans (page 34)
¾ cup liquid from cooking beans
½ cup bacon drippings or lard
1 cup jack cheese, grated

Follow the directions in above recipe for Frijoles Refritos, then stir in liquid. Beans should be creamy, not soupy. Just before serving add cheese and let it melt.

CHILE CON FRIJOLES

Chile with Beans

This is a quick chile that can be made on the spur of the moment, if the beans are already prepared. Besides serving as a main dish, it is also delicious on hot dogs.

This is my family's favorite chile. Whenever I change the recipe, my husband and son are always the first to notice. "She's at it again, Dad," or "Esther, we like it just the way it is," they protest.

- 1 pound ground beef
- ½ cup chopped onion
- 5 cups cooked pinto beans
- 3 tablespoons chile powder
- ½ teaspoon garlic powder
- ½ teaspoon salt
- ¼ teaspoon ground comino

Brown meat. Add onions, beans, and seasonings. Simmer 30 minutes. If the chile is too soupy, thicken with one to two tablespoons of corn meal.

Serve with hot corn or flour tortillas or with rice.

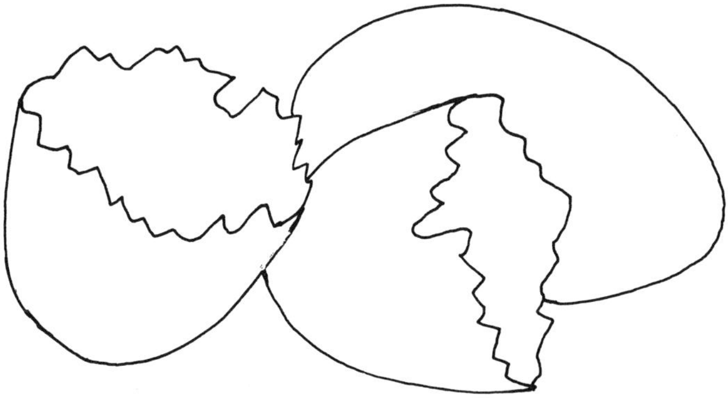

COMIDAS con HUEVOS
EGG DISHES

CHORIZO CON HUEVOS

Sausage and Eggs

⅓	cup water
8-12	chorizo sausages, or 1 recipe fresh chorizo (page 50)
1	medium onion, minced (optional)
4-6	eggs

Heat water in skillet. Skin sausage, if you are using commercially prepared sausages. Crumble sausage into skillet and cook until all of the water disappears. Add onion if desired and simmer 3 to 5 minutes.

Add beaten eggs and cook as for scrambled eggs. Or drop one whole egg at a time on the sausage and cook until eggs reach desired consistency. Or cook eggs separately and serve with sausage.

Yields 2 servings of Chorizo con Huevos.

Note: Prepared chorizos are available in many stores.

HUEVOS RANCHEROS

Ranch Style Eggs

My husband loves his Huevos Rancheros and would have them for a midnight snack as often as possible.

- 1 pound bacon
- 1 large onion, minced
- 3-4 small fresh green chile peppers
- 1 28-ounce can tomatoes, or 4-5 ripe tomatoes, minced
- 6-12 eggs
- salt to taste

Slice bacon in ½ inch squares and fry slowly until crisp. Remove bacon from skillet and sauté onion and chiles in bacon grease for 3 to 4 minutes. Add tomatoes and salt to taste. Bring to a fast boil. Add cooked bacon pieces and simmer for 5 to 10 minutes.

Carefully drop eggs into sauce and poach, covered. (The eggs may also be fried in a separate skillet and covered with the sauce when served.)

Serve with hot corn or flour tortillas. Yields 6 to 12 servings of Huevos Rancheros.

MEXICAN OMELET

2 tablespoons milk
2 eggs
1 tablespoon scallion, chopped
1 tablespoon chopped wax fresh chiles or chopped canned green chiles
1 tablespoon butter or margarine
salt and pepper to taste

Beat eggs, milk, salt, and pepper with fork, mixing well, then add the rest of the ingredients, except butter. Heat butter or margarine in skillet; be sure that it is hot but be careful not to burn.

Pour eggs into skillet, then turn heat to low. When mixture has set, lift and fold over, letting uncooked egg go to bottom of pan.

Cook eggs until done (about 5 minutes). Do not overcook; eggs should be moist.

Serves 1.

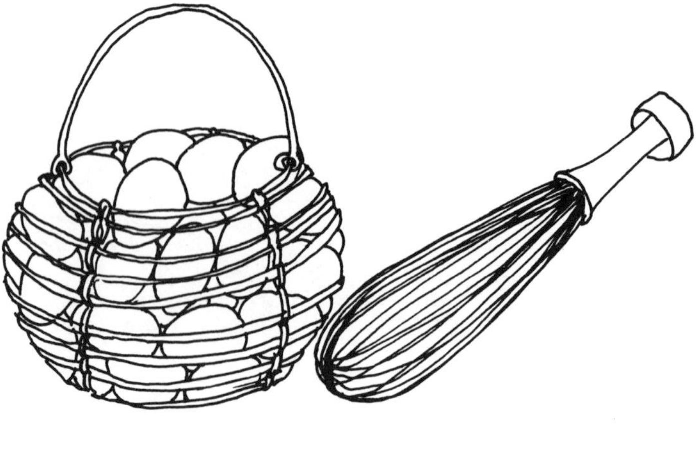

CARNE y COMIDAS
MEAT and MAIN DISHES

CHILE COLORADO

3 tablespoons lard or cooking oil
3 cups cubed stew meat, beef or pork
2 tablespoons flour
3 teaspoons chile powder or 4-5 tablespoons red California chile powder
1 large onion, chopped
1 clove garlic, crushed
¼ teaspoon ground comino
1 bay leaf
3 cups water
salt and pepper to taste

Brown meat in oil, add flour and brown, then add next 4 ingredients. Cook until onion is tender, then add water slowly, stir, bring to fast boil. Reduce heat, add bay leaf and simmer until meat is tender. Salt and pepper to taste. Serves 4-6.

Serve with rice, beans, and flour tortillas. This Chile Colorado can be used in making burritos.

Note: Ground California chile powder is not as hot as red chile powder and will make your sauce redder.

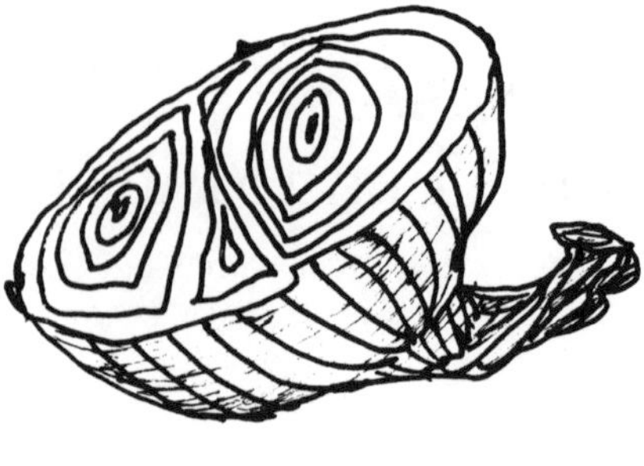

BURRITOS

Bean Burritos

large flour tortillas
minced onion
bacon fat
refried beans
jack cheese
lettuce
tomato, cut up
avocado, diced
jack cheese, grated
green onion, sliced

Warm tortillas in oven for 5 to 10 minutes. Sauté onion in bacon fat, add beans and cheese, heat together. Put one large spoonful of mixture in the center of each tortilla, top with lettuce, tomato, avocado, green onion, and grated cheese. Roll up the filled tortilla, folding up one end to prevent dripping.

Meat and Bean Burritos

1 package flour tortillas, large size, or make your own, page 78
refried beans, page 35
Chile Colorado, page 42

Place tortillas wrapped in foil in oven until warm.

Spread one half of the tortilla with beans. Add 1 tablespoon Chile Colorado, roll, then fold bottom up to prevent drips.

Serve hot; make sure that they are kept covered in a warm oven until all the Burritos are filled.

CHILE CON CARNE

Chile with Meat

- 6 long dried red hot peppers (California or Mexican chiles)
- 8 small dried red hot chile peppers
- 3½ cups boiling water
- ½ pound beef suet
- 3 pounds cubed lean beef
- 3 bay leaves
- 1 tablespoon comino seed
- 1 tablespoon fresh garlic
- ¾ teaspoon oregano
- 1 tablespoon sugar
- 1 tablespoon salt
- 1 tablespoon yellow corn meal
- 1 teaspoon ground black pepper

In a large bowl, cover chile peppers with boiling water and allow to stand for at least 30 minutes. Drain, saving both the water and the chiles.

Render all fat from the suet. Drain off all but ¼ to ½ cup of the fat. (Excess fat may be frozen for future use.) Sauté beef in reserved fat. Add 2½ cups of chile liquid. Bring to a boil. Add bay leaves and simmer for 45 minutes.

In blender, puree comino, chiles, remaining chile liquid, garlic, oregano, sugar, and salt. Pour over meat. Add corn meal to thicken. Simmer for 15 minutes.

Serve with hot corn or flour tortillas. Boiled rice or pinto beans may be used as a side dish.

Yields 10 servings of Chile con Carne.

TOSTADAS

It is very important that the oil be very hot in preparing the tortillas for this dish, or the tortillas will absorb the oil. Submerge the tortilla completely with the aid of a wooden spoon or other such utensil.

1	dozen tortillas
½	cup oil
4-6	cups refried beans, page 35
1	cup jack cheese, grated
½	head lettuce, shredded
2	diced tomatoes
1	avocado, cubed

Heat oil in frying pan until the top of the oil appears hazy, but not smoking. Fry one tortilla at a time until crisp and golden, but not brown. Set aside on a paper towel in a warm oven until all the tortillas are cooked.

Spread all of the tortillas with hot beans. Top with cheese, then lettuce, tomatoes, and finally, avocado. Serve with hot sauce if desired.

4 cups of beans will yield 12 Tostadas.

Note: I have made as many as 4 dozen tortillas for Tostadas ahead of time and had no problem. If you should want to prepare a number of tortillas ahead of time, use two skillets; it doesn't take as long. Sprinkle with salt as you drain them, then set aside in a dish or pan large enough to hold the amount you want. Cover with a dish towel. Remove the towel and heat pan in a preheated 350° oven for 15-30 minutes before assembling the Tostadas.

CAZUELA DE VERDURA

Vegetable Combination

If you like your vegetables hot, add 2 or 3 sliced green chile peppers to this dish while it is cooking, according to your taste.

2 tablespoons butter or margarine
1 pound zucchini, sliced
1 cup fresh or frozen corn
1 onion, diced
½ green bell pepper, diced
1-2 fresh tomatoes, peeled and diced
salt and pepper to taste
½ cup water

Sauté all vegetables in butter in skillet. Add water and simmer 15 to 20 minutes, covered. Season to taste. Serve hot.

Yields 4 to 6 servings.

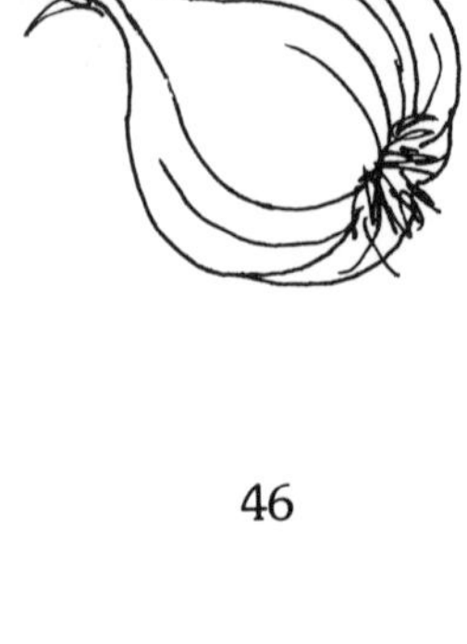

REPOLLO MEXICANO

Mexican Cabbage

While preparing this dish, you may prefer to add 2 or 3 sliced green chile peppers to make it hot.

1 tablespoon bacon drippings
1 head cabbage, cut in small chunks
1-2 fresh tomatoes, peeled, cut in large pieces, or 1 8-ounce can of tomato sauce
1 cup fresh corn
¼ green bell pepper, diced
½ cup water
salt and pepper to taste

Sauté all vegetables in bacon drippings. Add water and simmer, covered, for 15 to 20 minutes. Season to taste. Serve hot.

Yields 4 to 6 servings.

CHILES RELLENOS

Stuffed Chiles

If you do not want to use fresh chile peppers to make Chiles Rellenos, use the canned green roasted, peeled peppers.

12	fresh green chile peppers
4	eggs
¼	teaspoon cream of tartar
8	tablespoons flour
1	teaspoon salt
1½	pound block of jack cheese
½	cup oil

Wash chiles and pat dry. Rub with oil, then roast in 375° oven for 15 minutes or until chiles have become blistered. Place them in a paper bag or cover with a damp cloth and let stand for at least 15 minutes. Peel skin off, and make a small opening in side of each chile. Brush seeds out. (Leave them in if you want a hotter taste.)

Beat egg whites, adding cream of tartar, until stiff. Slowly fold in 5 tablespoons of flour. Beat egg yolks slightly and fold into above mixture.

Cut cheese in 3-inch by ½-inch strips. Place one strip of cheese inside each pepper. Roll filled chiles in a mixture of 3 tablespoons of flour and 1 teaspoon salt. Dip in egg batter. Fry in hot oil until golden brown. Remove and drain any excess oil on a paper towel. Place in warm oven until ready to serve.

Add sauce if desired (page 49).

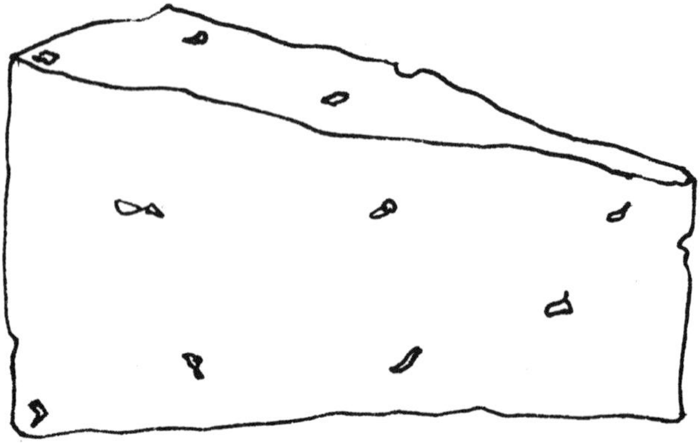

REPOLLO RELLENOS

Stuffed Cabbage

- 8 cabbage leaves
- 6 cups boiling water
- 1 teaspoon salt
- 4 eggs, separated
- ¼ teaspoon cream of tartar
- 5 tablespoons flour
- 1 can green chiles, sliced
- 8 1-inch x 5-inch strips of jack cheese
- 2 cups oil for frying

Separate leaves from cabbage with care. Steam leaves as follows: Put them in a kettle, pour 6 cups of boiling salted water over them, cover tightly, and let stand until ready to use.

Beat egg whites, add cream of tartar, and beat until stiff. Slowly fold in flour, then fold in slightly beaten egg yolks.

Place one strip of chile and one of cheese lengthwise on a cabbage leaf and roll up, fastening with a toothpick. When all cabbage leaves are stuffed and rolled, dip and roll each in batter, making sure that each is fully coated.

Fry 2 or 3 at a time in hot oil until golden brown. Remove and place on paper towel. Keep warm until ready to serve.

Serve with sauce, below, if desired. Serves 4-6.

Sauce

- 2 cups water or chicken broth
- 2-3 chicken bouillon cubes
- ¾ cup juice from can of whole tomatoes, or ¾ cup tomato juice, plus 1 whole tomato diced
- ¼ cup diced bell pepper
- ¼ cup diced onion
- 4 teaspoons corn starch

Add diced vegetables to liquids. (Add bouillon cubes only if you are using water.) Bring to a fast boil, reduce heat, add corn starch mixed with a little cold water, and simmer until onion and pepper are tender. If sauce is too thin, add a little more corn starch.

CHORIZO

Mexican Sausage

1 pound lean pork, coarsely ground
1 teaspoon salt
2 tablespoons chile powder
1 garlic clove, crushed
1 teaspoon oregano
2 tablespoons vinegar

Mix all ingredients thoroughly. Store in glass or crockery container in refrigerator.

Yields one pound Chorizo.

Note: This fresh Chorizo should be used right away, or within a week at the longest.

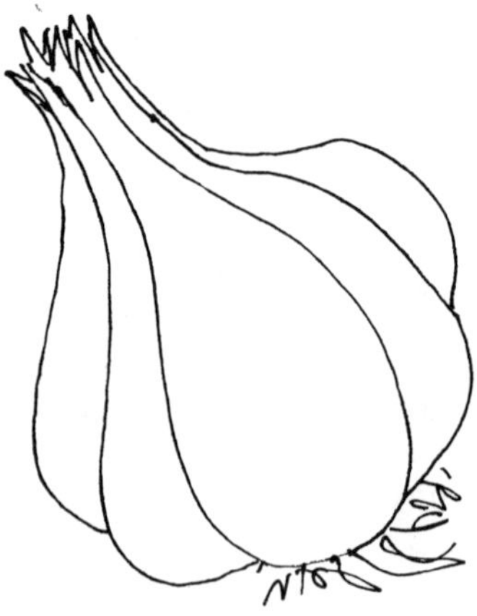

SUIZO BIFTEK A LA MEXICANA

Mexican Swiss Steak

- 4-6 green chiles
- 1 garlic clove or ⅛ teaspoon garlic powder
- 1 teaspoon salt
- ½ cup flour
- 2 pounds steak
- 3-4 tablespoons lard or oil
- 1 onion, finely diced
- 1 16-ounce can of tomatoes

Grind green chiles in molcajete with fresh garlic and a little water. Set aside.

Combine salt, flour, and garlic powder (when not using fresh garlic). Tenderize steak and cut to desired serving pieces, then dredge meat with flour. In heavy skillet heat lard or oil, and brown meat on both sides. Lower heat and add remaining flour, if any. Mix well, then add the rest of the ingredients. Cover and cook over low heat for one hour or until meat is tender. Add one cup water if it is too dry.

Serve with rice, beans, and flour tortillas.

Yields 6-8 servings.

TACOS

1 dozen tortillas
1 cup corn oil
½ head lettuce, shredded
2-3 tomatoes, chopped
½ cup cheddar cheese, grated
¼ cup onion, minced
meat filling, on next page

Hard Tacos

Fry one tortilla at a time in very hot oil, immediately forming a U-shaped center fold by holding one side of the tortilla with long-handled tongs and folding it over a wooden spoon. When the side in the oil becomes crisp, turn it over and continue to hold with the tongs until the other side is golden and crisp. Be careful not to burn it.

Fill the prepared tortilla with meat, lettuce, tomato, cheese, and onion. Red chile sauce may be sprinkled on the top if desired.

Hard tortilla shells may be purchased in many supermarkets if you do not wish to make your own.

Makes one dozen Tacos.

Soft Tacos

Dip corn tortillas, one at a time, in hot oil for no more than one minute. Drain off excess oil on paper towels. Cover and keep warm in oven.

After the tortillas are prepared, fold and fill with meat, lettuce, tomato, cheese, and onion. Red chile sauce may also be sprinkled on top if desired.

Makes one dozen Tacos.

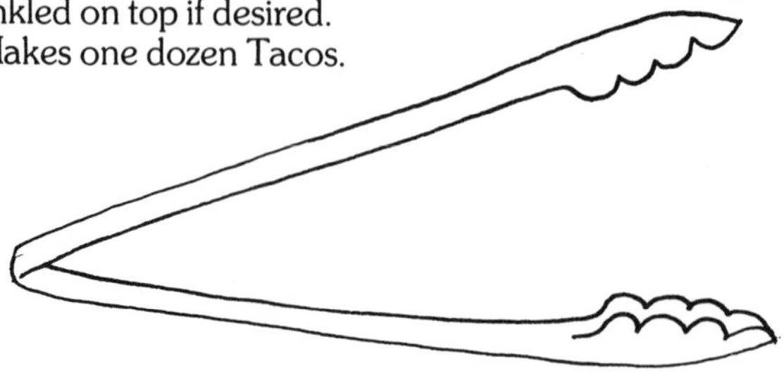

Meat Filling

1 pound ground beef
2 tablespoons oil
4-5 teaspoons flour
½ teaspoon garlic powder
1 teaspoon black pepper
1 teaspoon salt
½ teaspoon ground comino
½ cup water

Brown meat in oil, then add flour. When flour has browned, add other dry ingredients. Mix well, then add water. If too thick, add a little more water. Simmer for ten minutes. Keep covered and warm until ready to use.

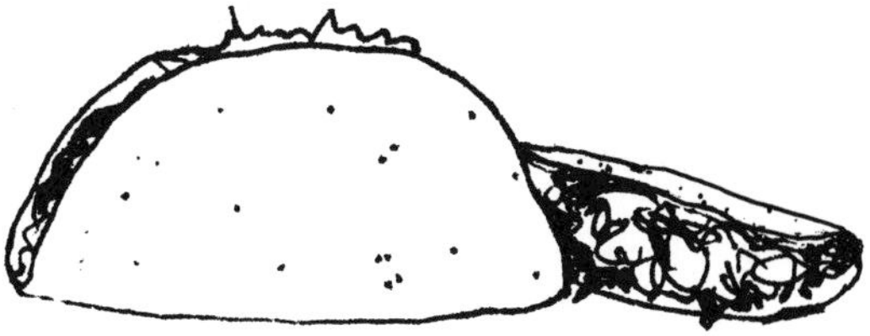

GUACAMOLE TACOS

This is a good way to use leftover pork.

2 cups shredded cooked pork
salt and pepper
12 corn tortillas
1 cup corn oil
guacamole, page 21

Shred and season pork. Heat.

Dip all corn tortillas in hot oil, as in making enchiladas (page 66). Drain on paper towels.

Place shredded pork at the end of a tortilla. Roll ¾ of the way and hold with an inserted toothpick. Fry in hot oil until crisp. Keep warm in oven.

Spread one tablespoon of guacamole on the remaining ¼ of the tortilla.

Makes 12 Tacos.

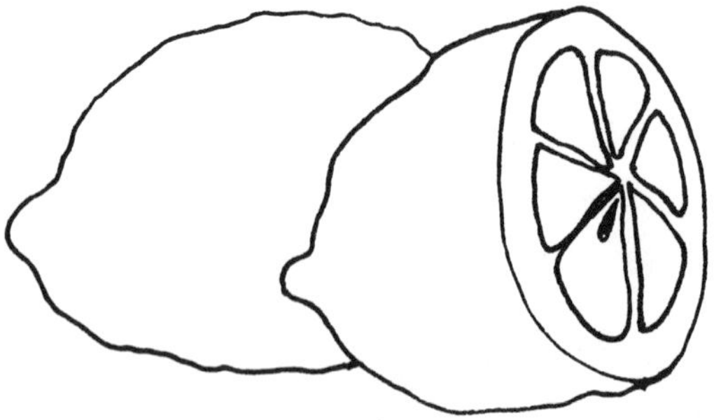

TAMALES

Esther's Tips on Tamales

Your first experience in making tamales may be a little frightening. It was for me. My mother wasn't there to help. Halfway through, I was ready to give up. Later I realized it wasn't that difficult. There is a lot of work involved, however, so I suggest that the first time you try it, you invite a friend or two and ENJOY making them as a project.

The real work involved with making tamales is spreading the masa. It will be unlike anything you have done before, but don't despair! By the time you have spread a dozen or two corn husks, you will acquire a feeling for it. If the masa is too sticky, add a little more broth to the mixture. If not, wet the masa as you spread it.

The first time I made tamales, I decided to use more masa during the spreading procedure, thinking that the more I used, the faster it would go. When I cooked my first batch, I ended up with fat tamales. Use only the amount of masa called for in the recipe, unless you would like to try fat ones. Some people prefer them that way, but I prefer them thin.

This probably seems like a large recipe to you. We usually make large numbers of tamales at a time, but you can cut the recipe in half. Tamales can be frozen or they can be kept in the refrigerator for a week. When reheating them, it is very important to reheat them in salted water. Otherwise, they will lose some of their flavor.

TAMALES

Tamales are very good for breakfast with a cup of hot sweet coffee. (Sorry, no cream!) If you cannot obtain corn husks in your area, parchment paper can be substituted. For information about whipping lard, see Esther's Helpful Hints, page 14.

- 7 pounds fresh picnic shoulder, salted to taste
- water
- 6 cups whipped lard or bacon drippings
- 4 tablespoons salt
- 6¼ ounces red chile powder
- 10 pounds fresh masa, medium texture (see note below)
- 3 cups broth from pork
- 15 garlic cloves
- 4 tablespoons comino seeds
- 5 tablespoons white flour
- 1 tablespoon black pepper
- 2 cups water
- 8-9 ounces No. 1 grade corn husks

Cook pork in a large pot for 1½ hours, adding enough water to cover. Save the liquid.

Mix lard, 3 tablespoons salt, 6 ounces red chile powder, and masa with 3-4 cups broth from pork. Knead masa until it feels smooth, about 20-25 minutes. Cover with a warm, damp cloth and set aside.

Note: When using instant masa follow directions on package, but instead of using plain water add the broth that the meat was cooked in. If there isn't enough broth, add plain water. For information about using instant masa, see Glossary, page 16.

Grind garlic cloves and comino in molcajete or with a mortar and pestle, adding a small amount of broth.

Mix flour and 1 cup broth. Dice pork, but do not mince. Combine diced pork, 1 tablespoon salt, pepper, garlic and comino mixture, and flour mixture in a skillet and simmer for 10-15 minutes. If you want to make some of the tamales extra hot, set aside enough meat for at least 2 or 3 dozen tamales and add 4 or 5 tablespoons red hot crushed peppers to the meat.

Most corn husks are already cleaned when purchased, but clean them again under warm running water. Soak in boiling water for at least 30 minutes, keeping covered with hot water at all times.

Taking a few corn husks at a time, wring out water and pat dry with a paper towel. To each corn husk add 1 tablespoon of the masa mixture and spread clockwise. If the masa becomes too sticky for spreading, add a little water or dip the spoon in water each time you spread.

In spreading the mixture make certain it is spread on the smooth side of the corn husk. Spread the mixture from side to side ¾ of the way down the husk, leaving ¼ of the husk free at the bottom. Add 1 tablespoon of meat and roll the husk. Fold the bottom up.

Place some of the corn husks that were too small to use and 2 cups of water in a deep pan. Place the molcajete upside down in the center of the pan (any round heavy heatproof object may be substituted for the molcajete or you can build your pyramid inside a colander and then set the colander inside the pot). Stand the tamales, one at a time, around the molcajete, building a pyramid until all of the tamales are used.

Cover with a damp cheesecloth and steam over low heat for one hour. The tamales will be done when the husk separates from the dough. Allow to cool before eating.

Tamales may be frozen. To reheat add enough water to cover the bottom of the pan with 1 teaspoon salt. Cook over low heat.

Yields 10 dozen tamales.

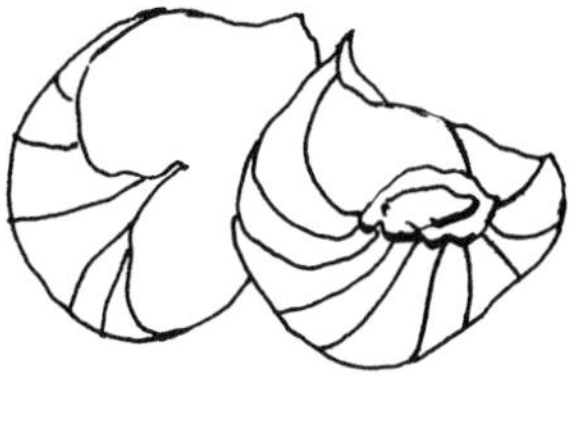

TORTAS

Tortas are delicious filled with meat left over from making tamales.

1 cup corn oil
2 pounds fresh masa
cold water
2-3 cups diced chicken, pork, or other meat
beans, lettuce, tomato, rice

Add enough cold water to masa so that the dough does not stick to your hands. Form into balls the size of golf balls. Pat into patties 5 inches in diameter and ½ inch thick. Cook, one at a time, on a hot, lightly greased skillet for one minute on each side. Keep the Tortas warm until all are finished.

Fry the cooked tortas, one at a time, in hot oil for three minutes. Drain on paper towels and keep warm.

With knife, make a slit one quarter of the way around the side of the Torta. Insert the knife in the slit and carefully cut inside of the Torta, forming an envelope-type opening.

Fill with meat, or with beans, lettuce, tomato, rice, or all of these combined.

Tortas Made with Bolillos

Bolillos are small rolls like French rolls. Tortas are made with these also.

6 bolillos
2 cups meat of your choice or beans
2-3 tomatoes, chopped
½ head lettuce, shredded
1 avocado, sliced
salsa of your choice
salt to taste

Cut rolls lengthwise and remove center. Fill according to your taste. The salsa can be added to taste.

GALLINA EN MOLE

Chicken Mole

If you do not want to make your own Mole (MO-lay) Sauce for this recipe, it can be found in some supermarkets in either liquid or powder form.

1	cut-up chicken
	water
1	teaspoon salt
2	tablespoons lard or bacon drippings
2-3	cups Mole Sauce (page 76)
1½	teaspoons sesame seed

Cover chicken with salted water, bring to a fast boil, and simmer for 30 to 40 minutes. Reserve broth for use in preparing sauce.

Prepare Mole Sauce according to the recipe.

Brown chicken in lard or bacon drippings. Cover with Mole Sauce and simmer for 15 to 20 minutes. Sprinkle with sesame seeds and serve.

Yields 6 servings of Chicken Mole.

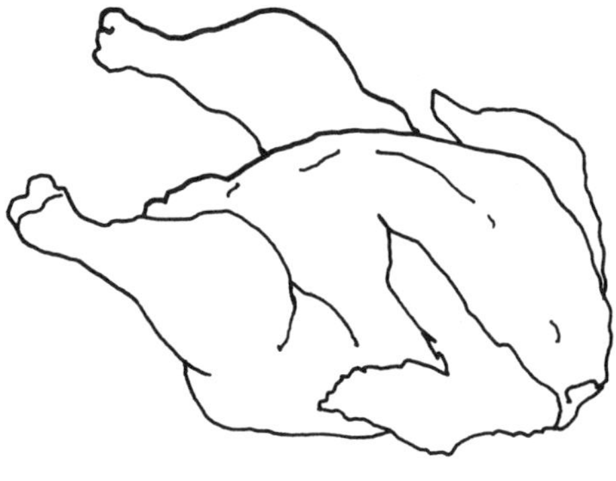

EMPANADAS

Dough:

- 3-4 ounces whipped lard (see page 14) or shortening
- ½ teaspoon salt
- 3 cups all-purpose flour
- 2 large eggs; 3 if medium size
- ½ cup milk

Add flour and salt to the whipped lard and mix well, then add eggs. Mix thoroughly. Add milk, a little at a time, and stir. Dough should be smooth. Put a little flour on the board and knead lightly until dough no longer sticks to hands.

Place in a bowl and cover. Let stand 30 minutes or place in refrigerator for 45 minutes. Form into one-inch round balls and roll on well-floured board.

Fill with any desired filling (pages 61-63), at least 2 tablespoons for each Empanada. Moisten edges with cold water. Fold dough in half, forming a half-moon shape. Pinch and press edges tightly, making sure ends are sealed. Fry in deep hot oil until golden brown, or bake in preheated 375° oven for 15 minutes or until brown. Drain fried Empanadas on paper towel.

PICADILLO FILLING

Mexican Mincemeat for Empanadas

1 pound ground beef
1 onion, chopped
1 garlic clove, crushed
1 tablespoon butter
1 8-ounce can tomato sauce
½ cup seedless raisins
1 tablespoon sherry (optional)
½ teaspoon ground cloves
1 teaspoon salt
1 tablespoon sugar
1 tablespoon cider vinegar

Brown meat, onion, and crushed garlic in butter. Add tomato sauce, raisins, sherry, cloves, salt, sugar and vinegar. Cook over low flame for 45 minutes.

Picadillo may also be served as a main dish.

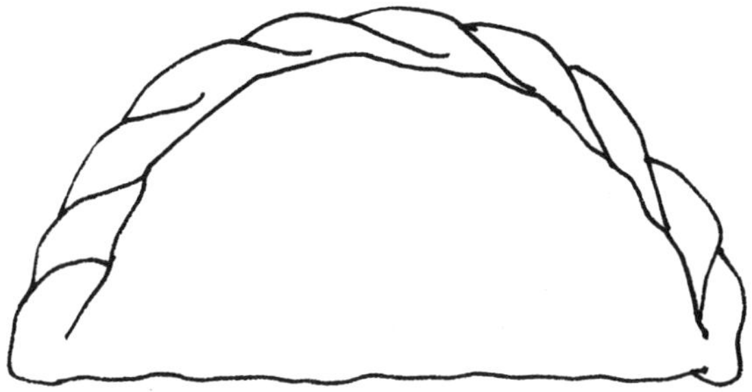

BEEF FILLING

for Empanadas

½ cup green bell pepper, chopped
1 chopped tomato
¼ cup onion, chopped
2 tablespoons oil
1 pound round steak cut into ½ inch cubes, or ground beef
⅛ teaspoon garlic powder or 1 garlic clove
⅛ teaspoon comino
salt and pepper to taste
½ cup stock or water

Sauté green pepper, tomato, and onion in oil until tender. Brown the meat with the pepper, tomato, and onion. Add the seasonings and water.

Cook for 30 minutes or until meat is nice and tender.

PORK FILLING

for Empanadas

1 tablespoon butter or margarine
2 cups cooked pork, chopped
¼ cup green pepper, chopped
¼ cup onion, chopped
1 tablespoon red chile powder
1 tablespoon flour
¾ cup broth from pork or water
salt and pepper to taste

Melt butter. Add pork, pepper, onion, and chile powder. Sauté for 5 minutes. Combine flour and broth, then add to mixture and simmer for 20 minutes. Salt and pepper to taste.

SEAFOOD FILLING

for Empanadas

- 1/3 cup butter
- 8 ounces cooked lobster, coarsely chopped
- 8 ounces cooked shrimp, coarsely chopped
- 8 ounces cooked crab meat
- 1/3 cup sherry
- 3 tablespoons butter
- 3 tablespoons flour
- 1 1/4 cup milk

Melt 1/3 cup butter. Add lobster, shrimp, and crabmeat. Mix well. Add sherry. Cover and set aside.

In another pan melt 3 tablespoons of butter. Add flour and cook 3 to 4 minutes over low heat. Slowly add milk. Bring to a boil. Pour over seafood and cook for 5 minutes.

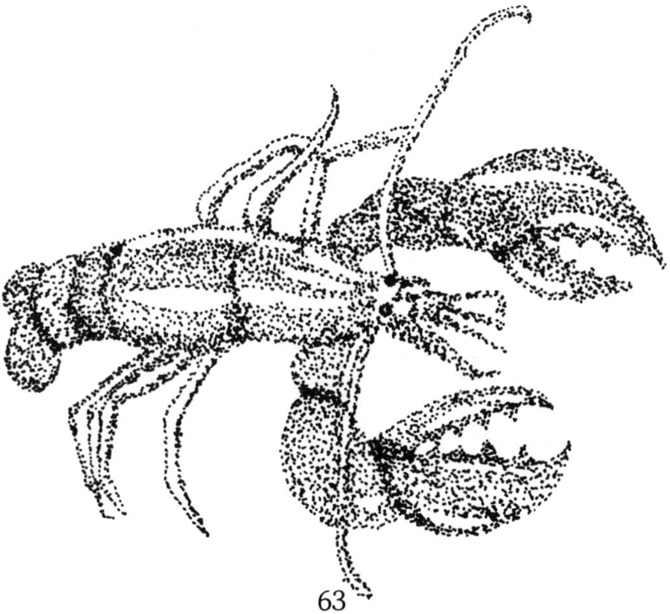

ENCHILADAS DE APIO

Celery Enchiladas

I have many other recipes for Enchiladas, but the ones I have included in this book are my very favorites.

- 1 dozen corn tortillas
- 1 can condensed cream of celery soup
- 1 cup water
- 2-3 cups grated mild cheddar cheese
- 1 minced onion (optional)
- 3 4-ounce cans roasted and peeled green chiles
- ½ cup oil

Preheat oven to 350°. Combine soup with water and the juice from the green chiles. Set aside. (This is to be poured over the enchiladas after they have been prepared.)

Mince onion and grate cheese. Set aside. Tear green chiles into wide strips. Set aside.

Heat oil in skillet. Quickly dip all of the tortillas, one at a time, into the hot oil. Fill each tortilla with 2 tablespoons cheese, one tablespoon onion, and ½ of a shredded green chile. Roll and arrange in a 9" x 12" baking dish.

Pour the soup combination over the enchiladas. Place any remaining chiles, cheese, and onion on top of the soup mixture. Cover tightly with aluminum foil and bake in preheated oven for 30 minutes. DO NOT OVERBAKE.

Makes 12 Enchiladas de Apio or 6 servings.

ENCHILADAS DE AGUACATE

Avocado Enchiladas

4 fresh wax chiles or 3 cans peeled roasted chiles
8 ounces sour cream
2 ripe avocados
½ teaspoon lemon juice
½ teaspoon salt
2 cups grated jack cheese
1 small onion, minced
12 tortillas
½ cup corn oil

Preheat oven to 350°.

Roast chiles, peel and shred (see page 49). Blend avocados well with sour cream, add lemon juice. Salt to taste and cover. (If canned chiles are used, shred lengthwise.)

Mince onion and grate cheese. Set aside. Dip tortillas, one at a time, in hot oil. Fill each tortilla with 2 tablespoons cheese, 1 tablespoon onion, and ½ of a shredded green chile. Roll and arrange in a 9" x 12" baking dish. Cover with sour cream and avocado mixture.

Bake in preheated oven for 15 to 20 minutes. Yields 6 servings of Enchiladas de Aguacate.

ENCHILADAS ROJAS

Red Enchiladas

Let me share with you my number one favorite enchilada recipe.

1	dozen corn tortillas
1	onion, chopped
2-3	cups grated cheddar cheese
3	tablespoons flour
3	tablespoons bacon drippings
2	beef bouillon cubes
1	teaspoon salt
½	teaspoon garlic powder
½	teaspoon ground comino
2	tablespoons red chile powder
1-2	cups boiling water
½	cup oil

Preheat oven to 350°. Chop onion and grate cheese. Set aside.

Brown flour in bacon drippings until almost burned. Remove from heat. Add next five ingredients. Mix well and return to heat. Slowly add water, stirring to a smooth red sauce. Simmer gently while preparing other ingredients, adding more water if the sauce becomes too thick.

In another skillet, heat oil. Quickly dip the tortillas, one at a time, into the hot oil and then into the enchilada sauce. NOTE: The tortillas must be dipped into the oil and removed very rapidly in order to prevent them from becoming rubbery.

Fill each tortilla with 2 tablespoons cheese and 1 teaspoon onion. Roll and place side by side in a 9" x 12" baking dish. Pour remaining sauce over enchiladas. Sprinkle with remaining cheese and onion.

Cover and bake in preheated oven for 20 minutes. Enchiladas must be covered tightly to prevent the edges of the tortillas from becoming hard. DO NOT OVERCOOK.

Makes 12 Enchiladas Rojas or 6 servings.

ARROZ
RICE

ARROZ CON CAMARÓN

Rice with Shrimp

1	garlic clove
¼	cup oil
2	cups uncooked rice
¼	cup chopped onion
½	cup tomato sauce
½	pound cooked shrimp
¼	teaspoon Spanish saffron
	salt and pepper to taste
1½	cup water

Sauté garlic in oil until it reaches a golden color. Discard garlic. Sauté rice in oil until brown. Add onion, tomato sauce, shrimp, saffron, salt and pepper, and water, adjusting the amount of water to the amount required on the rice package. Cover and simmer 30 minutes or until all liquid has been absorbed.

Yields 6 to 8 servings of Arroz con Camarón.

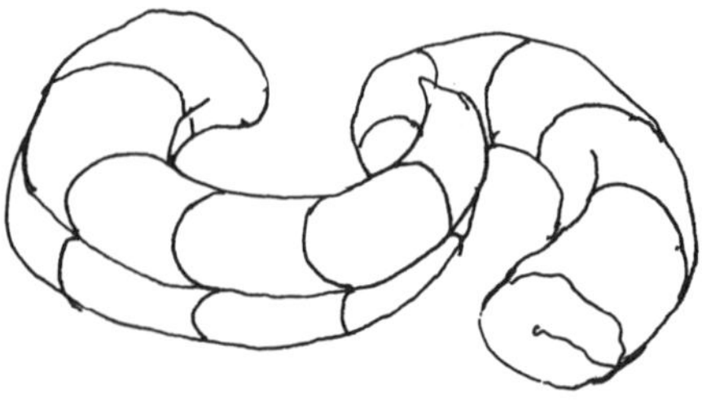

ARROZ CON POLLO

Chicken with Rice

1 frying chicken, cut up
2 tablespoons butter or margarine
6 servings Mexican Rice, page 70
salt and pepper to taste

Wash chicken and pat dry (chicken may be skinned if preferred). Brown in butter or margarine, but do not overcook.

Place Mexican Rice in skillet (an old-fashioned black iron skillet is preferable). Add chicken and cover. Cook on low heat for 30 to 40 minutes, adding salt and pepper to taste.

You might want to use the unused chicken pieces such as wing tips, neck, etc., to prepare your own chicken broth called for in the Mexican Rice recipe.

Yields 6 servings of Arroz con Pollo.

MEXICAN RICE

In preparing Mexican Rice, canned chicken broth may be used, but NEVER USE PLAIN WATER.

- 2 cups raw rice
- 3 tablespoons bacon drippings
- ¼ teaspoon ground comino
- ½ teaspoon black pepper
- ½ teaspoon garlic powder
- 2 cups chicken broth
- salt to taste
- 4 rings sweet bell pepper
- 2 slices onion

Brown rice in bacon drippings until very dark, being careful not to burn it. Allow rice to cool for a few minutes. Add broth and seasonings. Mix well. Cook according to the directions on the rice package. Adjust the amount of chicken broth to the amount of liquid required in the directions on the rice package.

Arrange bell pepper rings and onion slices on top of the rice. Do not stir.

Serves 4.

RED RICE

2 cups rice
2 tablespoons bacon drippings
¼ teaspoon comino
½ teaspoon black pepper
½ teaspoon garlic powder
1 cup chicken broth
1 cup tomato puree or chopped tomatoes
salt to taste
4 rings sweet bell pepper
2 slices onion

Sauté rice and seasonings in bacon drippings for three minutes. Add chicken broth and tomatoes or puree. Mix well. Cook according to the directions on the rice package. Adjust the amount of chicken broth to the amount of liquid required in the directions on the rice package.

Arrange bell pepper and onion on top of rice. Do not stir.

Serves 4.

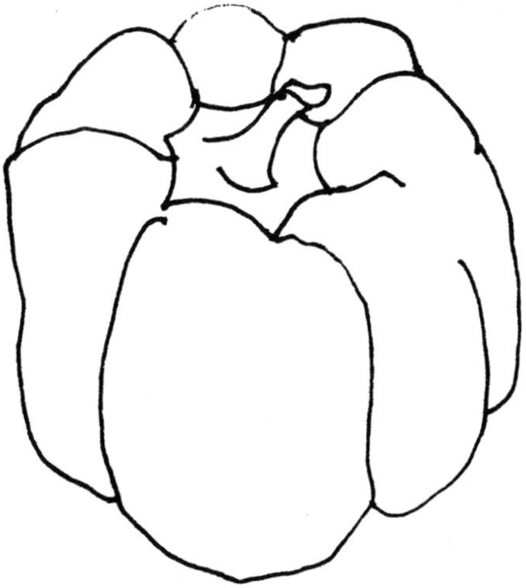

ARROZ BLANCO

White Rice

I hadn't fixed this dish for some time, so this morning I cooked it to test my old recipe, and I gave a taste to my son. He loves rice and is my expert rice-tester. After the taste, his comment was, "How about a bowl, Mom?" That was all the convincing I needed, and I included the recipe.

- 3 tablespoons lard
- 1¼ cup uncooked rice
- 1 small onion, minced
- ¼ teaspoon ground comino
- ¼ teaspoon garlic powder
- salt and pepper to taste
- 2¾ cup chicken broth, or 2¾ cup water with 3 chicken boullion cubes

Heat lard, add rice, onion, and all spices. When onions have become transparent, add broth. Bring to a fast boil, reduce heat, cover, and simmer for 20 minutes or until all liquid is absorbed.

Serves 4-6.

SALSAS
SAUCES

SALSA CRUDA

Chile Sauce

This sauce may be served as a dip for Tostada Chips or as a relish with meals.

- 2-3 hot peppers (yellow wax or serrano)
- 1 small onion, minced
- 2 ripe tomatoes, or 1 cup cooked tomatoes, minced
- 1 teaspoon salt
- ½ teaspoon minced garlic clove
- ½ teaspoon oregano
- ½ teaspoon comino seed
- 1 teaspoon lemon juice (optional)
- 1 tablespoon fresh cilantro, minced
- 1 tablespoon cider vinegar

Roast peppers over flame and peel (see instructions, page 15). In molcajete, grind peppers, salt, garlic, oregano, and comino seed. Add small amounts of the minced tomatoes and onion, continually grinding, until all of the tomatoes and onions are used.

As a last resort, a blender may be used instead of a molcajete, but caution should be used not to blend these ingredients more than ½ to 1 minute.

Combine ground ingredients with freshly chopped cilantro and vinegar. If the Salsa Cruda is too hot, add lemon juice. The vinegar serves as a preservative which makes cooking unnecessary. Keep refrigerated at all times.

Yields 1½ to 2 cups of Salsa Cruda, or Chile Sauce.

SALSA VERDE

Green Chile Sauce

3-4	tomatoes or 1 16-ounce can tomatoes
2-3	California chiles
1	small minced onion
1	teaspoon salt
1	teaspoon vinegar
2-4	serrano chiles

Peel and chop tomatoes. Mince or grind the chiles in molcajete, then add the rest of the ingredients.

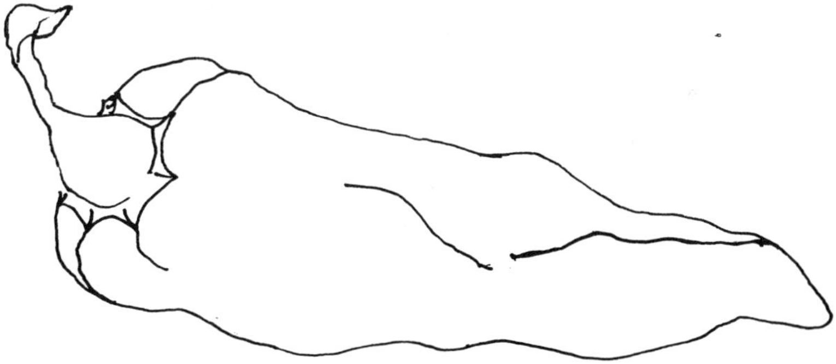

MOLE SAUCE

2 cups hot chicken broth
3 dried Pasilla chiles
3 dried Mulato chiles
3 dried Ancho chiles
1 cup raw or unsalted peanuts
¾ cup minced onion
2 medium tomatoes, peeled and seeded
1 garlic clove
½ teaspoon cinnamon
½ teaspoon sugar
½ teaspoon anise seed (optional)
½ teaspoon salt
½ teaspoon coriander seed (optional)
½ cup raisins
3 squares unsweetened chocolate

Remove seeds from chiles under cold running water. Pour boiling hot broth over chiles, soaking them for 30 minutes.

In blender, puree chiles and broth, then add all of the remaining ingredients except the chocolate and the anise seeds.

Cook puree in 2 tablespoons lard or bacon drippings in skillet for 3 to 4 minutes. Add chocolate and simmer until all of the chocolate is melted.

Anise seeds are to be added to the sauce just prior to combining the sauce with the poultry or meat.

Yields Mole Sauce for 6 servings.

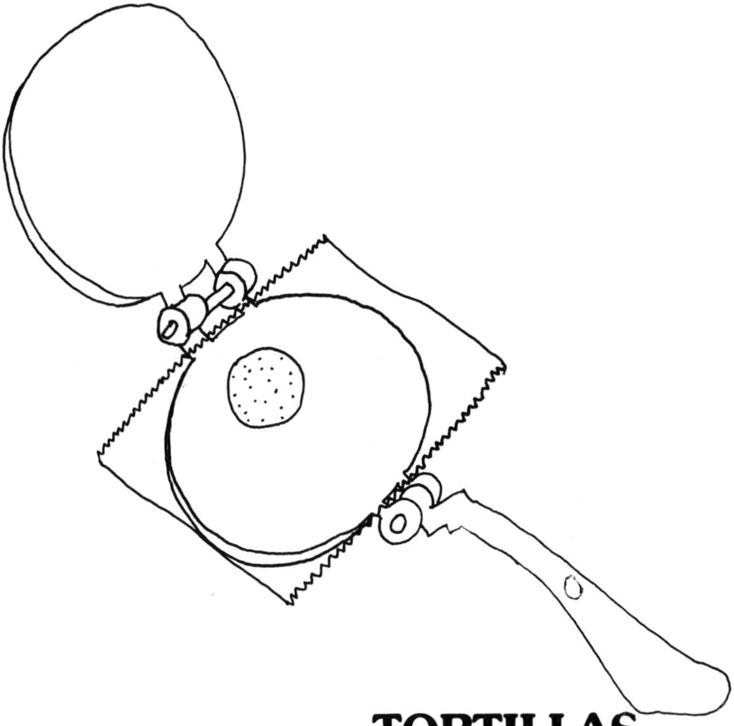

TORTILLAS

FLOUR TORTILLAS

When making flour tortillas, use lard if possible; they will be much tastier and softer. There have been times that I have not used lard but oil in making tortillas. When my mother comes to visit, she will not eat my tortillas if I do not use lard.

- 3 cups self-rising white flour
- ⅓ cup lard or oil
- ⅔ cup hot (not boiling) water

Mix flour and lard or oil. Add water. Work the mixture well by hand until it is the consistency of fresh dough. The dough should not stick to your fingers.

Take a small piece of the dough, the size and shape of a golf ball, and form into a patty. Roll out with a rolling pin.

Each time you roll the tortilla, pick it up, twisting it to the right, then roll again. You probably will not get the tortilla round the first few times you try, but cook it anyway. It will taste just as good.

Cook the tortillas on a *comal* (a black iron griddle) or, if that is not available, in a black iron skillet. Heat the ungreased comal or skillet until a drop of water skips across the surface. Place the tortilla on comal, cook about 1 to 2 minutes, turn and cook other side the same length of time. The tortilla should be a light golden brown when done. Keep warm in oven, covered.

Flour tortillas may be frozen and reheated in the oven later. They may be served with any Mexican dish or eaten hot with just butter. They may also be filled with any meat and eaten as a taco.

Yields one dozen Flour Tortillas.

FLOUR TORTILLAS FROM SCRATCH

3 cups all-purpose flour
1½ teaspoons baking powder
1 teaspoon salt
⅓ cup corn oil or bacon drippings
1¼ cups lukewarm water

Sift flour, baking powder, and salt through your fingers. Add corn oil or bacon drippings and mix thoroughly with your fingers until the mixture is crumbly, with fine lumps, resembling pie dough.

Add the water a little at a time, mixing thoroughly. Dough will be ready to knead when it does not stick to your hands. Knead for one minute.

Proceed as in recipe for Flour Tortillas, page 78.

Yields one dozen Flour Tortillas from Scratch.

CORN TORTILLAS

2 cups masa harina (instant masa)
1 cup water

If you wish to use fresh masa, it may be purchased at a *tortilleria* (tortilla factory). Do not add water if you are using fresh masa.

Combine masa harina and water. Knead until well blended. If the dough does not hold together very well, add a little more water.

Shape into 12 balls (or fewer). Press between two sheets of wax paper with a tortilla press or by hand. Bake on lightly greased griddle until brown on both sides.

These are very good with just butter, and may be served with any Mexican dish.

Yields one dozen Corn Tortillas.

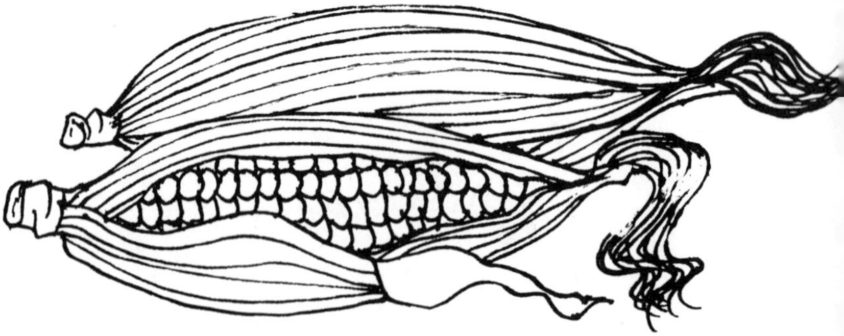

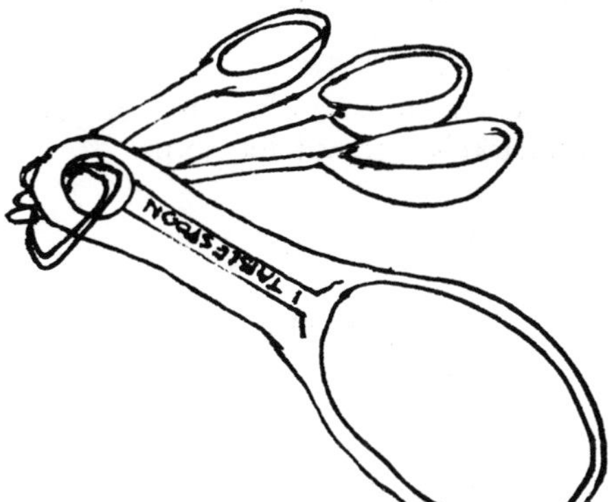

POSTRES
DESSERTS

BUÑUELOS

The Dessert

Try these topped with cheese and honey. I think you'll find them interesting and delicious.

1 package large flour tortillas
¾ cup corn oil
honey
cinnamon
sugar
½ cup finely grated jack or cheddar cheese

Fry tortillas, one at a time, in hot oil until golden brown and crisp. Drain on paper towels.

Sprinkle with one of the following:

1. Honey
2. Cinnamon and sugar
3. Grated cheese and honey. When the cheese is melted from the heat of the tortilla, top with the honey.

Serve hot.

New Years Dessert

2½ cups flour
½ teaspoon baking powder
½ teaspoon salt
2 eggs
¾ cup water or milk
¼ cup butter or margarine
1 cup oil

Sift dry ingredients together. Beat eggs, butter, and milk together. Add to flour mixture. Proceed as in making tortillas, page 78. Roll out very thin.

Fry in hot oil on both sides until golden brown. Sprinkle with sugar, cinnamon, or cheese and honey.

Yields 24 Buñuelos.

CAMOTES FRITOS

Fried Sweet Potatoes

To make this into a delightful holiday dish, add ¼ cup raisins and ¼ cup chopped pecans.

6 medium sweet potatoes or yams
¼ pound margarine or butter
2 cups brown sugar or piloncillo (see Glossary)

Peel sweet potatoes. Slice lengthwise and cut in strips as in cutting French fries.

In heavy skillet, melt butter and sugar. Add sweet potatoes. Cook over low heat until golden brown. DO NOT OVERCOOK, or they will get mushy.

Yields 6 servings of Camotes Fritos.

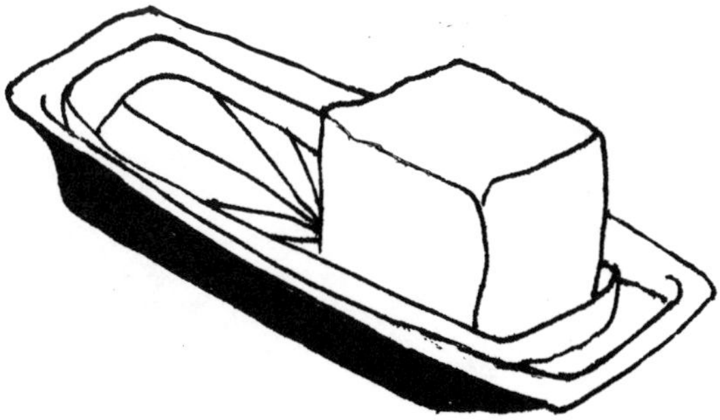

CAPIROTADA

Bread Pudding

Capirotada is delicious served hot, but may be served cold as well.

- 8 tablespoons melted butter
- 12 slices bread, toasted
- ½ cup raisins
- 1 pound longhorn cheese
- 1½ cups brown sugar or 3 small piloncillo loaves
- 2 cups hot water
- ¼ teaspoon ground cloves
- ¼ teaspoon cinnamon
- 1 cup chopped walnuts or pecans (optional)
- 3-4 sliced bananas (optional)

Preheat oven to 325°. Dip toasted bread in butter. Alternate layers of bread with the raisins, cheese, nuts, and bananas in a baking dish. It is not necessary to remove the crusts from the bread except for appearance's sake, so I suggest you remove them only when you want to be fancy!

Boil sugar, water, cinnamon, and cloves until the sugar dissolves. Pour over the pudding. Bake in a preheated oven for 15 to 20 minutes, or until a knife inserted in the pudding comes out clean.

Yields 12 servings.

SWEET TAMALES WITH FRUIT

- 3 pounds fresh masa
- 2 teaspoons baking powder
- dash of salt
- 1½ cups sugar
- 2 cups whipped lard (see page 14)
- 1 teaspoon cinnamon
- 1 teaspoon vanilla
- 1 cup raisins
- 1 20-ounce can crushed pineapple with syrup
- 1 box sun-dried apricots (follow directions on box for stewing; add 3 tablespoons sugar)
- 1-2 cups masa harina

Combine masa, baking powder, salt, sugar, lard, cinnamon, and vanilla. Mix well. Then add fruits and syrup from fruits. Only if the masa becomes runny or mushy, add masa harina until smooth and not sticky. It is not necessary to add all the masa harina.

Spread mixture on corn husks that have been cooked in boiling water for at least an hour. Place open corn husk on palm of hand, then add 1½ tablespoons mixture to husk. Do not spread as for regular tamales; just fold up husk at middle and then fold each side to the center. Place tamales in steamer, standing them on end in a circle. Cover with wet cloths and cook for approximately 2 hours or until the husk and masa are not sticky. These tamales can also be made in the same manner as meat tamales: Spread masa on husk, add fruit, roll, fold bottom up, place in pot standing up, cook.

CHOCOLATE MEXICANO

Mexican Hot Chocolate

Delicious served with Mexican pastries.

4 cups milk
4 tablespoons unsweetened cocoa or 4 squares unsweetened chocolate
½ cup sugar
½ teaspoon cinnamon or 4 cinnamon sticks
pinch of salt
½ teaspoon vanilla

Combine cocoa and milk in sauce pan, adding milk slowly until cocoa is dissolved. Add sugar, cinnamon, and salt. Heat over low flame, stirring constantly as you would for pudding, until almost boiling. DO NOT SCALD.

Remove from heat and add vanilla. Beat with egg beater until frothy. Serve.

Makes 4 cups of Chocolate Mexicano.

An instant Chocolate Mexicano can be found in some grocery stores in Mexican communities. It comes in round blocks, divided into sections. It is already sweetened and flavored with cinnamon.

Dissolve one quarter of a block of Mexican Chocolate in one cup of milk. Heat just to the boiling point. Beat until frothy.

Yields one cup.

Note: Mexican stick cinnamon is different in texture and taste from that which we buy in the United States. In making Chocolate Mexicano our cinnamon is a disappointment to the connoiseur, but as a substitute, it still makes a delightful cup of chocolate.

MEXICAN MOCHA

2 cups milk
2 tablespoons unsweetened cocoa
2 tablespoons sugar
dash of salt
⅛ teaspoon cinnamon
2 tablespoons instant coffee
whipped cream

Mix cocoa, sugar, and salt in a small glass, add a small amount of milk and stir to make a smooth paste.

Scald milk, then add cinnamon, coffee, and chocolate paste; mix well. Pour into individual cups and top each with whipped cream.

If a stronger coffee flavor is desired, add one more teaspoon instant coffee per cup. If you do not want to use instant coffee, use freshly perked coffee—one cup coffee to one cup milk.

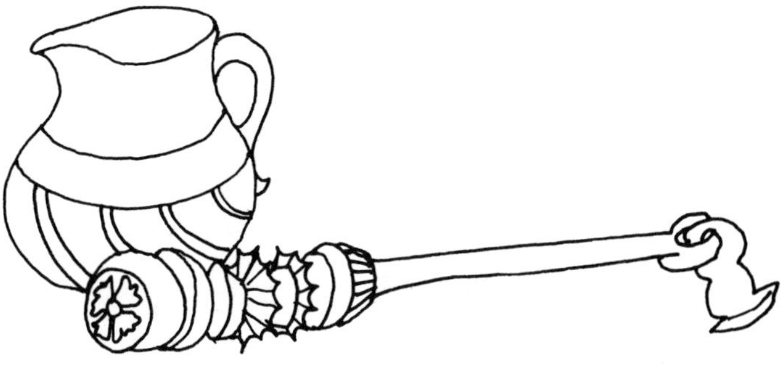

DESSERT EMPANADAS

Dough:

- 3-4 ounces whipped lard or shortening
- 3 cups flour
- 3 tablespoons sugar
- 2 large eggs, 3 if medium size
- ½ cup milk

Add flour to the whipped lard and mix well, then add sugar and eggs. Be sure to mix thoroughly. Add milk, a little at a time, and stir. Dough should be smooth. Sprinkle a little flour on board and knead lightly until dough no longer sticks to your hands.

Place in a bowl and cover. Let stand 30 minutes or place in refrigerator for 45 minutes. Form into one-inch balls and roll on well-floured board.

Add filling, page 89, at least 2 tablespoons for each Empanada. Moisten edges with cold water. Fold dough in half, forming half-moon shape. Pinch and press edges tightly, making sure ends are sealed. Fry in deep hot oil until golden brown; if you prefer to bake them, place in preheated 375° oven for 15 minutes or until brown. Drain the fried Empanadas on a paper towel.

Serve hot or warm. May be served with ice cream or topped with whipped cream.

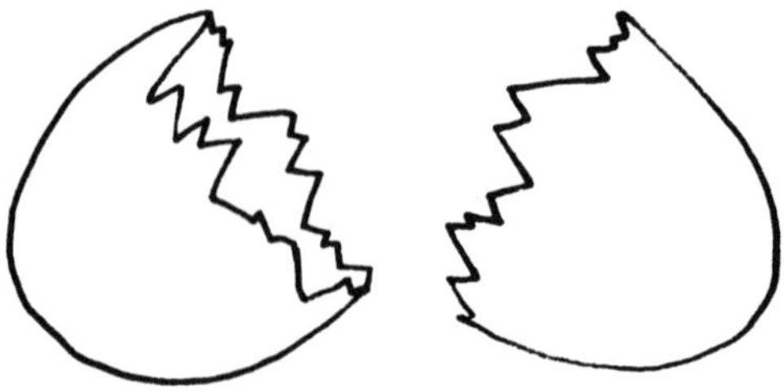

PUMPKIN FILLING

for Empanadas

2 cups canned pumpkin
1 teaspoon cinnamon or 1 teaspoon pumpkin pie spice
¼ cup brown sugar
¼ cup raisins (optional)
¼ cup chopped pecans (optional)
1 tablespoon butter

Combine all ingredients and cook over medium heat, stirring at all times. As soon as it comes to a boil, remove from heat and cool before using.

SWEET POTATO FILLING

for Empanadas

2 cups cooked mashed sweet potatoes
¾ cup brown sugar or to taste
1 tablespoon butter
dash of salt

Melt butter, then add sugar. Be sure sugar has dissolved before adding sweet potatoes. Add salt and mix well. This filling can be used right away.

FRESH FRUIT DESSERT

1	fresh pineapple
2-3	fresh papayas
2-3	fresh mangoes
	fresh limes

Slice fruit, wedge lime, and arrange on serving dish. The lime is for squeezing over the papayas and mangoes; one lime wedge per person is sufficient.

This is a very light dessert and is excellent for serving after dinner. It can be prepared ahead of time; do make sure, however, that it is kept tightly covered until serving time.

POLVORONES

Mexican Tea Cookies

2 cups flour
¾ cup butter
1½ teaspoons vanilla
⅛ teaspoon salt
4 teaspoons water
½ cup confectioners' sugar, for rolling or dusting baked cookies

Cream butter and add salt, vanilla, and sifted flour. Blend well, then add water. Form into a ball and chill for 2 hours.

Just before using, let stand at room temperature for 15 minutes. Divide dough into 2 balls and roll gently on a lightly floured board until about ¼ inch thick. Dough will resemble pie crust. Cut into one-inch squares or with a cookie cutter into one-inch circles.

Bake in 350° oven for 12 to 15 minutes. After cookies have cooled, roll in or dust with powdered sugar.

Yields approximately 4 dozen cookies.

SOPAIPILLAS

Fried Sweet Bread

How do they taste cold? All right, but there are never any left over in our home. They disappear as fast as I can make them.

2 cups all-purpose flour
¼ teaspoon salt
1 tablespoon baking powder
5 tablespoons sugar
1 tablespoon shortening
¾ cup milk
1 cup oil (for deep frying)
powdered sugar, honey, butter (for final step)

Sift all dry ingredients together. Cut in shortening as you would in making pie crust. Slowly add milk. Turn out on lightly floured board and knead gently until dough is of a smooth consistency. Cover and allow to rest for 45 minutes to an hour.

Roll out as for tortillas, then cut into small squares about ¼ inch thick. Heat oil to about 380° to 400°. Drop squares, a few at a time, into the hot oil. When pieces start to puff up into little pillows, turn at once. Keep turning to brown both sides to a golden color. Drain on paper towels.

Sprinkle with powdered sugar, or make a small opening in the sopaipilla and pour in a little honey. Butter if desired.

Note: Roll out as many as you can at first. If you need to stop to roll some more, turn heat to simmer and just before dropping pieces in, turn back up to high. When you have done this a few times you will be able to judge your heat without taking readings on the thermometer.

PLATANITOS

Fried Plantains

3	medium plantains, sliced
1-1½	cups brown sugar
¾	cup margarine or butter

In heavy skillet, melt margarine or butter and brown sugar. Add plantains and sauté over medium heat until golden brown.

May be also served as a side dish or snack.

FLAN

Caramel Custard

Caramel coating:

Heat a heavy skillet; pour into it ½ cup sugar. Stir constantly with a wooden spoon until all sugar is melted into a golden honey-colored liquid; be careful not to burn. Remove at once and pour into pan or mold. Swirl to coat bottom and sides of pan, and set aside.

Custard:

- 3 cups evaporated milk
- ½ cup sugar
- dash salt
- 3-4 eggs
- 1 teaspoon vanilla

Combine first three ingredients in pan, bring to a fast boil. Reduce heat and simmer for 15 minutes. Remove from heat, strain, and set aside to cool. When cool, add slightly beaten eggs and vanilla and mix well, then strain again. Pour mixture into caramelized dish, and place this dish into a larger pan of hot water. Bake at 350° for about 45 minutes, until a knife inserted in the custard comes out clean. Remove from oven immediately; cool before serving.

Flan may be inverted onto platter or spooned from baking dish into serving dishes. Pour some of the caramel sauce over each serving.

The outer pan of water is very important in baking this custard, as it will maintain an even temperature around the Flan while cooking.

To order more copies of

A TASTE OF MEXICO

Enclose a check for $3.95 for each copy plus $.95 shipping for 1 book (add .30 shipping each additional book), payable to Rand Editions/Tofua Press.

California residents add .24 tax per book.

Please send ________ copies of A TASTE OF MEXICO to:

Name ____

Address ____

____

I enclose a check for ____________________ (including tax if applicable)

Please charge my ______ Mastercharge ______ Visa

Card number ______________________________________

Expiration date ____________________________________

Rand Editions/Tofua Press

10457-F Roselle St., San Diego, CA 92121 (714) 453-4774

To order more copies of

A TASTE OF MEXICO

Enclose a check for $3.95 for each copy plus $.95 shipping for 1 book (add .30 shipping each additional book), payable to Rand Editions/Tofua Press.

California residents add .24 tax per book.

Please send ________ copies of A TASTE OF MEXICO to:

Name ____

Address ____

____

I enclose a check for ____________________ (including tax if applicable)

Please charge my ______ Mastercharge ______ Visa

Card number ______________________________________

Expiration date ____________________________________

Rand Editions/Tofua Press

10457-F Roselle St., San Diego, CA 92121 (714) 453-4774

Cookbooks by Rand Editions/Tofua Press

MICROWAVE COOKING MY WAY: It's a Matter of Time,
by Grace Wheeler, $8.95
(Calif. tax .54 per book; shipping 1.30 per book)

THE ELEGANT HORS D'OEUVRE, A Collection of Hors d'Oeuvre Recipes for Conventional and Microwave Cooking
by Margon Edney and Ede Grimm, $5.95
(Calif. tax .36 per book; shipping .95 for 1-2 books)

FOOD WITH A FLAIR: Special Recipes for Special People,
by Doone Lewis, $4.95
(Calif. tax .30 per book; shipping .95 for 1-2 books)

A TASTE OF MEXICO, A Primer of Mexican Cooking,
by Esther Gonzales Davis, $3.95
(Calif. tax .24 per book; shipping .95 for 1-2 books)

DINNER IN THE MORNING,
A Collection of Breakfast and Brunch Recipes,
by Elizabeth N. Shor, $3.95
(Calif. tax .24 per book; shipping .95 for 1-2 books)

Master Charge or Visa accepted;
include card number and expiration date.